S0-BBZ-962

Peace Works

Young Peacemakers
Project Book II

Holliston Public Schools
Extended Day Program
Linden St.
Holliston, MA 01746

Kathleen M. Fry-Miller
Judith A. Myers-Walls
Janet R. Domer-Shank

Illustrations by
Janet R. Domer-Shank

Foreword by
Ronald C. Arnett

BRETHREN PRESS
Elgin, Illinois

Peace Works:
Young Peacemakers Project Book II

Copyright © 1989 by Kathleen Fry-Miller, Judith Myers-Walls, and
Janet Domer-Shank

BRETHREN PRESS, 1451 Dundee Avenue,
Elgin, Illinois 60120

All rights reserved. No portion of this book may be reproduced in
any form or by any process or technique without the written con-
sent of the publisher, except for brief quotations embodied in criti-
cal articles or reviews.

Cover design by Jeane Healey
Cover illustration by Linda French Griffin
Illustrations by Janet R. Domer-Shank

Library of Congress Cataloging in Publication Data

Fry-Miller, Kathleen M.
        Peace works.

        Includes index.
        Bibliography: p.
        Summary: Includes instructions for a variety of projects that
promote peace and concern for the environment.
        1. Peace—Juvenile literature. 2. Environmental protection—
Juvenile literature. [1. Peace. 2. Environmental protection] I. Myers-
Walls, Judith A. II. Domer-Shank, Janet R. III. Title.
JX1963.F869 1989   327.1′72   89-970
ISBN 0-87178-977-9

Manufactured in the United States of America

To our parents

whose example

planted the seed,

and whose support

helped it to flourish

Contents

Foreword

Passing on the promise that a better world is possible to the next generation of peacemakers is a needed task. We need to offer to the next generation a practical vision that embraces a sense of responsibility calling them to make a difference, to swim against the current if needed in order to give peace a chance. Such a peacemaking vision is needed in a world where cynicism about whether we can make a difference and lack of sensitivity to global and environmental issues too often foster attitudes of indifference and inhibit a commitment to people, institutions, and values.

Making a Difference

Theologian and philosopher Jacques Ellul has stated that one of the major problems of the latter part of the twentieth century has been the "eclipse of the self." People do not feel empowered to make a difference. As peacemakers we need to "pass on the promise" that an individual life is important enough to make a difference. The notion of the "sanctity of life" requires that a peacemaker respect the unique contribution each individual brings to human community. Peacemaking rejects the form of violence that discourages another from making a creative difference with a life. Peacemaking begins as people recognize that each person is not only sacred as individuals, but needs to be afforded the opportunity to make a difference, to contribute to the human community.

Lack of confidence in our ability to affect the future can lead to despair. Such an attitude is at odds with the peacemaker's fundamental call to hope. As we work on tasks together there is a sense of hope that a life of peacemaking can make a difference. As the Biblical scholar Walter Brueggemann suggests such a hope reminds us that we are all of one people, one tribe, one family, inviting all to prosper in God's community.

A Realistic Hope

We need to embrace a sense of hope within a realistic value structure that can sustain community. Ethicist Stanley Hauerwas positions hope within the context of patience, courage, hope, and charity. Any effort at peacemaking that encourages us to make a difference needs to assume the backdrop of patience, courage, and charity in order to avoid our efforts at making a difference giving way to cynicism from expectations not met. Hauerwas reminds us that hope cannot be unduly optimistic. Cynicism is not given birth by our only working with little, but rather from undue expectations that we optimistically believe we will achieve, determining only too late that our goals were unattainable from the beginning. In essence, cynicism is given birth from mindless optimism.

Life needs to be lived between the extremes of undue optimism and a lack of hope in the future. Such a middle road suggests that the human being can make a difference, but not without some toil and struggle. To pass on the promise of hope within a realistic context of courage, patience, and charity to the next generation requires finding ways to make a difference with their work and faith, while avoiding naive optimism.

Peace Works

Peace Works: Young Peacemakers Project Book II by Kathleen Fry-Miller, Judith Myers-Walls, and Janet Domer-Shank follows this important tradition of keeping hope alive and well in a practical and realistic fashion, as the project book gives young people concrete ways to make a difference. Children learn hope from their work with the scriptures, life together from the witnesses of other peacemakers, and from the discovery that they, too, can make a difference. Hope is kept alive by faith and by practical and realistic actions of peacemaking.

The books are a guide for children on how to make a difference, how to be peacemakers in everyday living. Children and adult leaders will be instructed in practical ways to work with the sun, the seasons, jobs, toys, festivals, and celebrations. *Young Peacemakers* reveals that "what can be" is limited only by what we can envision and develop in a practical way. The authors nourish "hope" of peacemaking by passing on to the next generation the baton of concern for the earth and others through the involvement of adults and children in practical peacemaking tasks. Perhaps life is best when practical tasks bring people together in hope, cooperation, and accomplishment for their community. It is this spirit of practical peacemaking that has inspired the content of the *Young Peacemakers* books.

The activities suggested by the authors involve work and effort on the part of young people and leaders. The project book requires nothing beyond what can be accomplished in short settings, but is work nevertheless. One important way of revealing that we can make a difference for the long-run of life is to introduce themes such as work and patience at a young age. The *Young Peacemakers* books do a good job of bringing together the theme of making a difference in a context that will encourage hope, not mindless optimism.

This book reveals that peace can work and young people can learn to make a difference in everyday living. Peacemaking and hope begin with and are tested more often in the performance of small daily tasks than in the ordeal of a major glorious mission. The *Young Peacemakers* books simply remind us that we are called to make a difference as peacemakers and such a task can begin at home in our practical work together with one another. Such a message is needed for young people and is an important reminder for all peacemakers as we try to make a difference with our work and life together.

Ronald C. Arnett
North Manchester, Indiana

Introduction

Making Peace with Fun, Celebration, and Hope

Peacemaking is serious business. War, toxic waste, poverty, and other examples of violence are sobering topics. Although these issues cannot be ignored or belittled, an important aspect of peacemaking is the art of celebration. Peacemaking is more than building a just society and righting wrongs; it is the skill of approaching daily life joyfully and holding a positive attitude toward the future. Because children often fear death and loss (including nuclear war and nuclear accidents), because hope is the best gift adults can give children as they fend off societal and developmental threats, and because children simply love celebrations, positive and playful experiences must be a part of adults' efforts to teach peace to children.

In our first book, the *Young Peacemakers Project Book,* we provided ideas for activities to help young people aged three to ten begin to explore and understand issues of preservation of the environment, social justice and appreciating and accepting diversity, conflict resolution, and commercialism of violence and holidays. In this book we deal with many of the same issues, but from a primarily playful perspective.

In our writing we make several assumptions. First, we believe that peace is not the absence of conflict, but rather a way of dealing with conflict that enhances all those involved in the conflict instead of demeaning or degrading them. We also believe that *all* life is valuable, including human, animal, and plant life and any combination of them. In connection with that concept, we feel it is important for adults and children to broaden the boundaries they draw around their world. The larger the area they consider "home," and the more people and other living things they consider as "family," the more likely it is that they will be peacemakers. Another basic assumption is that children are important for who they are and what they can contribute *now,* not only because they will be adults someday. Although this material is written for and directed toward children, we are not assuming that all of this is foreign or new to children and needs to be taught. Much of the knowledge and wisdom that will surface as a result of the activities will come from children who know and do many of these things already. Perhaps many adults will learn (or relearn) as much or more than children by participating. Closely related to the valuing of children is our belief that self-esteem is a basic building block for human development. Success teaches more than failure, and self-confidence leads to competence. The best activities are those that present a reachable challenge.

Finally, we believe it is important for adults and children to establish a dialogue about peace. Peace is like a number of other very important topics in that parents and other adults find it very difficult to know how and when to bring it up, so they avoid it. It is hard to know what young children will be able to grasp or what language to use to explain concepts. The activities contained here and in the first book provide shared activities, a language, and concrete experiences as a context for dialogue. Just as children need to learn the facts of life and death, they need to learn the facts—and the values and the emotions—of peace and war. If they can learn in an atmosphere of hope with respect for themselves and others, children can grow up with the confidence that they, and we, can have an impact on the world as we work for peace. Perhaps this book can be a start.

Play is a Child's Work

The explosion of knowledge about children and child development that has occurred in recent decades has resulted in a major shift in adults' understanding of the function of play in children's lives. While in the past play was seen as simply frivolous entertainment, it is now understood that children learn through play. They use the nonthreatening atmosphere to experiment with objects, people, and ideas. They learn cause and effect, sequence, size relationships, and social skills. They can experiment with adult skills and behaviors in a setting in which they themselves are in charge. They can control the laws of time and become anyone and anything they want to be.

The verdict concerning war play is not so clear-cut, however. Some experts believe war play is an important part of childhood and that children need the opportunity to be powerful and explore life and death. Others believe that war play may have served that function in the past, but that current war toys, children's violent TV programs, and the international climate have changed the picture for children. Yet others believe that war play simply should be banned because it encourages competition, destruction, and hurting others in the name of fun.

In this book we take a stance that discourages the use of either commercial or child-created war toys and encourages alternatives to war play without ignoring children's developmental needs. We feel that most war toys on the market are not good toys; they leave very little to the child's imagination and many can be dangerous. We also are very concerned about the exploitation of children connected with many toys, most of which are advertised on Saturday morning television and on children's networks. We also are concerned that war toys have a "weapons effect" on children that suggests aggressive and rough play, and that such play can make it difficult for children to control their behavior and may inhibit cooperation and nurturance.

Children do need opportunities to feel powerful and to extend their influence over their environment. They need opportunities to be involved in active, exciting play and to experiment with strategy and problem solving. Rather than accomplishing that with guns, shooting, bombs, swords, knives, and fists, we encourage the use of flashlights and hoses, picking up heavy objects or doing other heavy "jobs," and learning to use words. All extend the influence of the child beyond his or her hand. We encourage the excitement of fighting fires, dealing with pretend medical emergencies, and conquering the deprivation of a deserted island. We also encourage many creative activities that use art, music, drama, and creative interaction with nature to help to meet the needs of active, energetic children. Cooperative games also can provide exciting and powerful experiences for children; most are fast-moving and require the use of large muscles. More complex projects that extend or grow over a period of time can hold children's interest and anticipation; this is another aspect of "war play" for which these ideas provide an alternative. For those parents and teachers who do not want to ban guns and war play, this book offers at least some choices and some balance.

Children and Nuclear War

As a society we have much training in focusing on the negative, on problems, and on what is not going well. Society's approach to education about nuclear war has been no different.

Because of this, there has been special concern about the threat of nuclear war and the reaction of children and youth. The assumption had been that young people who were concerned about the future of the world would be filled with despair and hopelessness and have a sense of no personal future. Apparently this is not the case. Those children who express the most concern about the possibility of nuclear war tend to be those who also are most optimistic about being able to avoid the threat. Either adults have been pairing nuclear education with ideas for making a personal impact, or else those children most hopeful about the future also are most able to admit their fears. In either case, rather than being fearful of talking with children about the issues, we need to balance the threat and despair with hope and planning for the future.

About the Structure of this Book

Peace Works is structured to make it easy for children to take a lead in choosing the activity they would like to complete. The illustrations provide the child with an idea of what each activity involves. For the parent or teacher working with one or more children there is a background section at the beginning of each chapter that describes the importance of the activities in that chapter and their relationship to peace issues. The chapter introduction also includes the objectives which are addressed by the activities in that chapter. The text describing each activity has been written at a level that should be understandable to children aged three to ten when it is read to them. Older children in that age group will be able to read the words themselves.

There are really two types of activities described here. The first type comprises most of Chapters 1 and 2 and part of Chapter 3. These are discrete activities that result in a product or experiment. Children will be able to complete many of the tasks with a certain amount of independence; yet it is hoped that parents or teachers will join with the children to complete at least some of the activities cooperatively. Such involvement will both increase the effectiveness of the teaching and provide an opportunity for strengthening the adult-child relationships. We also believe that adults will enjoy the projects almost as much as the children! Those activities or steps of activities that require adult guidance for safety reasons or because the task is too difficult for children to accomplish on their own is marked with this symbol: *A* (for Adult).

The second type of activities are those which describe play themes or game, party, and celebration ideas. Many adults believe that children will get along fine on their own with such activities, but we again encourage parents and teachers to get involved. Professionals in early childhood education (as referenced in the publication *High Scope ReSource*) have offered some rationale and techniques for parents to get involved. Children left entirely on their own may hit a snag in their play and give up, they may be afraid to try new things and experiment, or they may turn to destructive behaviors out of frustration. Adults can help children avoid those pitfalls. Adults can play an important role by helping to create a rich physical environment that includes a variety of materials to stimulate creativity and imagination in play, and includes enough space for the play to take place. They can provide nonverbal support by watching, listening, participating, imitating, and getting on the child's physical level. Verbal support could include the kinds of things listed in the "Let's Talk About It" sections in addition to referring children to each other as resources and translating their activities into words (especially for young children) to make them aware of their actions. When participating in children's play, however, be sure to let them take the lead.

Appropriate Age Levels

These activities were designed for children aged three to ten years. We hope that most children of those ages will find the activities enjoyable and will be able to understand, or at least begin to understand, many of the ideas being presented. Activities which are definitely too difficult or otherwise developmentally inappropriate for most younger children are marked with this symbol: *O* (for Older child). Because the three to ten age range is a broad one, it is important to understand the differences among children of those ages and present the activities appropriately. For our purposes here, the children can be grouped roughly into three categories: preschool (approximately 3-5 years); early elementary (approximately 5-8 years); and late elementary (approximately 8-10 years).

Preschool children doing the discrete activities (Chapters 1, 2, and part of 3) should be given simple tasks that do not take long periods of concentration. They should be able to see immediate results and should not be required to do anything that involves complex skills. They will need close, step-by-step guidance and hands-on experiences that allow them to see, hear, touch, taste, and smell. Adults should be ready to help with the more complex aspects of the activity, but should not take over in the areas in which the child is competent. In their play, preschoolers will take on roles, but may not expand those roles in very many ways. They also may not stick with one role for a long period of time. They are likely to show a large amount of repetition in their play and are likely to want and enjoy realistic equipment and props. For both activities and play settings, a simple statement of the values and ideas behind the projects can be introduced, but adults should hold realistic expectations for how much preschoolers will understand. Listen carefully to their comments as they try to put these complex ideas into words that they can comprehend.

Younger elementary level children, on the other hand, will be able to be more independent with the projects. They will begin to be able to read some of the descriptions themselves and, perhaps, do some of their own writing. They will be able to plan for the projects by gathering materials, helping to prepare the work or play area, and working around the schedules of friends, classmates, and family. They are developing more skills and will be able to do more complicated tasks, but they still will need much guidance, especially when the task is new. Progress with discrete projects should be noticeable to these children in one or two sessions. They probably will use an increasing amount of creativity in their play, will stay in individual roles longer, and will interact in more complex ways as they play. At this age the "Let's Talk About It" questions can be especially helpful in leading the child toward an understanding of concepts behind the activities. Early elementary children may suggest some exciting alternatives to the written descriptions.

Older elementary level children will be able to read the project descriptions and will be able to complete many of the tasks with little or no adult instruction. They may want to do the activities entirely on their own, but we encourage parents and teachers to discover ways that the children can work and play beside the adults rather than under their supervision. Adults may need to help the children interpret what they are reading and help to make decisions about the appropriateness of the chosen activity considering available time and resources. Late elementary children will be able to grasp most of the concepts and values behind the activity; adults can help them explore those thoughts further and apply them to related situations. Children of this age also will be able to go beyond the activity to other projects of their own creation, will be able to think of alternative ways of completing the tasks, and will be able to think of implications beyond those represented in the "Let's Talk About It" sections. This can be an exciting time for the adults as well as for the young people!

Another important point related to age is that some of these activities provide a rich opportunity for working with multiple age groups. Cooperative games allow participants of widely varying ages and skills to play together. Older children can help the younger ones with some of the other tasks. Younger children can share their excitement and sense of wonder with the older ones. Older children can increase their understanding of the concepts by explaining them to the younger ones, which helps the younger ones, too. Young people who may feel they are "too old" to participate in the activities may benefit from helping to direct a younger group in their completion. Use caution in encouraging children of different ages to play together, however. Because play changes with age, younger children may find them-selves left out or left behind when the play is led by older children. At the same time, older children may manipulate younger ones to serve certain roles or functions in the play rather than allowing them to be full partners. Or the older ones simply may not use their full creativity if trying to accommodate the needs of the younger ones. Flexibility is the key; use your imagination and consult your own expertise in working with children.

About the Targeted Audience

Beyond being useful to different ages, this book should be useful to a variety of types of audiences. Families can use it for family activity times, for rainy days, and for times when little ones say, "I don't have anything to do." They may want to refer to it when war play becomes an issue. In these ways, parents may make it a part of their own peace education efforts.

Teachers, leaders, and other adults in nursery schools, child care homes and centers, after-school activity programs (including youth programs such as Scouts, Camp Fire, and 4-H), and public schools may find it provides just the thing for new approaches to energy, nature, and seasonal projects. It also could be a rich source of game, play, and party ideas for a variety of groups. Preschool and elementary school teachers may find that some activities can be used for interest areas, and others can be whole group activities.

About the Authors

Two of the authors are preschool teachers and the other is a college professor and Cooperative Extension specialist in the area of child development. We all have and work with children and parents and have used the activities included here in a variety of settings. We also all have roots in the Church of the Brethren, known as one of the traditional peace churches. Our commitment to peace involves a commitment to celebration, hope, and having fun. We hope the fun and excitement are contagious. May you enjoy making peace with children!

Kathleen Fry-Miller
Fort Wayne, Indiana

Judith Myers-Walls
West Lafayette, Indiana

Janet Domer-Shank
Dayton, Ohio

Section I
Fun With Nature

1
Nature Power

Background information:

This chapter addresses both issues related to caring for the environment and issues of justice. The control, understanding, and conservation of energy have become major peace issues in the world. Although the concern about an energy crisis comes and goes, the fact remains that the most commonly used fuels are non-renewable, obtaining them is difficult and has a potentially negative impact on the environment, and using them produces polluting waste. Traditional energy sources are not evenly distributed in countries or sections of countries. In addition, it is expensive for individuals to gain access to the energy. These situations set up conflict and power relationships that constantly challenge peace and justice.

Although this chapter does not introduce such abstract concepts as those outlined above, it does attempt to add to children's appreciation and understanding of renewable sources of energy. These include solar, wind, and water power. Sunshine and wind are two very difficult commodities for young children to understand. Neither can be held and manipulated, and wind itself cannot be seen. The activities in this chapter attempt to show children what wind and sunlight can do in order to help them begin to understand them. The power of wind, sun, and water and how that power relates to more conventional energy sources is demonstrated through the various activities. Children will not be likely to have an immediate impact on their environment in this area, but their beginning understanding of renewable energy sources may have a continuing impact as they grow older.

Objectives

For Young Children:
- To begin to understand that wind moves trees, flags, and other items, rather than the other way around.
- To experience the heat and evaporative power of the sun.
- To learn that water has the ability to move things.

For Early Elementary Children:
- To use some simple methods for harnessing the power of wind, sun, and water.
- To learn about some of the more sophisticated methods of harnessing renewable energy sources.
- To understand the basic difference between non-renewable and renewable energy sources.

For Later Elementary Children:
- To learn how methods of harnessing renewable energy sources work at a mechanical level.
- To plan ways to use renewable energy sources without sophisticated equipment.
- To explore the implications of the use of renewable energy sources for peace and justice.

For All Children:
- To identify the purpose of windmills, water wheels, dams, and solar collectors.
- To become aware of energy use in everyday activities.

Solar Power

Solar Snacks

Solar Tea

You Will Need:

- a glass jar   • a sunny day
- water, tea bags, and honey or apple juice and cinnamon

What To Do:

1. Sun Tea—Fill a glass jar with cool water. Add one or two herbal tea bags for a half-gallon container. Add a little honey, too, if you like. Apple Tea—Fill the jar with apple juice and a little cinnamon.

2. Put the lid on, but do not make it tight. Set the jar in the sun. Sun tea will take several hours. Apple tea should be done in less than an hour. (Do not leave apple juice or tea with honey in the sun for more than two hours. Enjoy your solar tea!

Sun-Dried Apples

You Will Need:

- apples, cut in half   • knife (safety knife for young children)
- a cutting board   • a cookie sheet   • a thin cloth   • a sunny day

What To Do:

1. Put apples on a cutting board, the flat side down. *A* Slice the apples with a knife—carefully.

2. Lay the slices on a cookie sheet and cover them with a thin cloth. Set the apple slices in the hot sun until you can bend them and they are chewy. It may take more than one day of sunshine. (If it does, bring them inside overnight.)

3. You can try other kinds of fresh fruits, also. Peach slices, pear slices, apricot halves, and pineapple slices are especially good.

Cheese Toast

You Will Need:

- bread   • slices of cheese   • a ziplock bag   • a sunny day

What To Do:

1. Arrange the cheese on top of the bread.

2. Put the bread and cheese inside the ziplock bag and close it. Then put the bag in the sun.

3. Watch the sun puff up the bag and melt the cheese. Eat your cheese toast! (Do not eat it if the bag melts.)

Hot Art

Solar Prints

You Will Need:
- colored construction paper
- some objects with interesting shapes

What To Do:

1. Lay your piece of construction paper in the sun. Arrange one or more objects on the paper.

2. Come back in several hours and take the objects away. See the picture that remains.

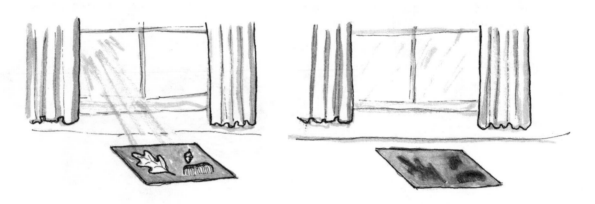

Water Painting

You Will Need:
- a cup of water
- a paint brush
- a sidewalk

What To Do:

1. Dip the brush in the cup of water. Paint pictures on the sidewalk.

2. Watch the pictures disappear with the sunshine!

O Wood Art

You Will Need:

- various pieces of wood
- magnifying glass

What To Do:

1. *A* Focus your magnifying glass to concentrate the sun's light through the glass on your piece of wood. It should look like a single, bright dot. Hold the dot still in one place until the wood starts to darken and smoke.

2. Slowly and carefully move your magnifying glass to "draw" on your wood. Keep your fingers away from the burning dot! It is hot!

3. As you practice wood burning art, you may want to draw a picture on the wood before you start burning it.

Some Like It Hot

Water Heater

You Will Need:

• a tub or plastic pool   • cold water
• a thermometer (or your hand)   • a sunny day

What To Do:

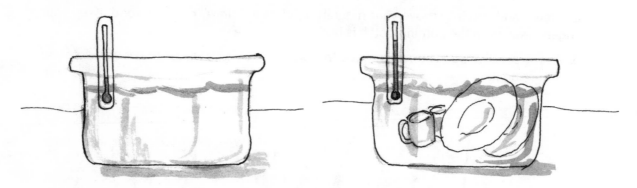

1. Fill your tub or pool with cold water. Check the temperature with the thermometer, or feel it with your hand.

2. Leave the water in the hot sun for a few hours.

3. Check the water temperature again. Feel if it changed. Use the water for playing, doing dishes, washing up, or whatever else you can think of.

Clothes Dryer

You Will Need:

• wet clothes   • a clothesline   • clothespins

What To Do:

1. Hang the wet clothes on the clothesline with clothespins.

2. Wait a few hours and check your things. Feel how wet or dry the clothes are.

Let's Talk About It:

What happens to the water in the fruit, in the sidewalk paintings, and in the wet clothes? What happens to the water in the tea and in the "water heater"? What makes those things happen?

Why is solar energy good for the earth? Why does solar energy take longer than machines to do some things?

How do people use energy from the sun for heat and light every day? What else uses solar energy? Think about plants and animals. What would the earth be like without the sun?

Why is sun energy called a renewable energy source? How is it different from coal, oil, nuclear, and other sources of energy? Does any person or country own the sun?

Other Things To Do:

Try using solar energy to do other jobs. Cook and dry other kinds of foods and fruits.

A Look in a library for instructions for making a more efficient solar oven. Try baking cookies in the oven you make.

A Visit a home or building that has solar collectors. What is the energy used for? How does it work?

O Find out the difference between passive and active solar systems. Think of ways you can use passive solar heating during the winter in your home, church, or school. Think of ways to avoid solar heating in the summer. Try some of those things. Do they make you feel more comfortable? Do they make your furnace or air conditioner work less often?

Windy Day Hike

You Will Need:

- a windy day   • crepe paper streamers or scarves

What To Do:

1. Go for a walk on a windy day. Take streamers or scarves on your walk to watch them "fly" in the wind. Hold onto one end and then let go to see how far the wind can carry your scarf or streamer. Be sure to collect your streamers after they fly. Watch where you are going!

2. While you walk, look for nature objects that can "fly" in the wind, too. You might find feathers, milkweed pods, or dandelion seeds. Watch for leaves, grasses, sand, snow, branches, and other things that move when the wind blows.

Pinwheels

You Will Need:

- a pencil with an eraser at one end
- a straight pin
- paper
- scissors
- crayons
- a ruler

What To Do:

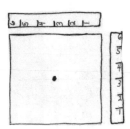

1. *A* Cut a piece of paper six inches square. Mark the center of the square.

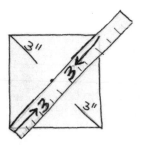

2. Lay a ruler diagonally from corner to corner of the square. Draw a line three inches long from each corner toward the center. Do the same thing at the other corners.

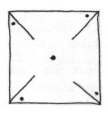

3. Mark dots near the corners as the picture shows.

4. Color pictures or designs on both sides of your paper. Cut along the lines.

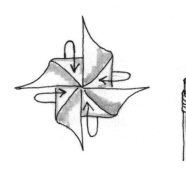

5. Bring together the corners with the dots at the middle. Stick the straight pin through the dots and into the eraser end of the pencil.

6. Use your pinwheel outside on a windy day or make your own wind by blowing into your pinwheel.

Bubbles

You Will Need:
- dish soap   • bowl   • water   • glycerin (from a drug store)
- paper cups   • wire or pipe cleaners
- straw loop—2 straws with a 2½ foot piece of string threaded through the straws and tied

What To Do:

1. Make bubble solution. Mix ½ cup dish soap, ¼ cup glycerin, and one gallon of water. Let it sit at least overnight.

2. Make bubble wands. You could cut the bottom out of a paper cup. Make a loop at the end of a pipe cleaner or short piece of wire. Or use a straw loop, a tea strainer, a funnel, or canning rings. Or try making giant bubbles by putting the solution in a wading pool and using a hula hoop.

3. Dip the bubble wand into the bubble solution. Hold it up and blow gently into the circle. Stay away from painted porches. The bubbles make it slippery!

4. See if you can hold up the wand and have the wind blow the bubbles. Watch how the wind current carries the bubbles away!

Let's Talk About It:

How does the wind feel? How does it sound? What can it do? You can not see the wind, but do things look different on a windy day? How are a gentle breeze and a big gust of wind different?

Why is wind called a "renewable energy source"? Is it a better source of energy in some places than in others, or at different times of the year?

How does the wind help plants? Why are dandelion seeds, maple seeds ("helicopters" or "whirly birds"), and milkweed pod seeds shaped the way they are?

Other Things To Do:

A Fly kites in the wind. You may want to get a kite kit or make your own kite using very thin, lightweight wood strips, string, and paper. Notice the direction of the wind when you fly your kite. Does it change?

Find out about and look for ways that people use wind energy. You might want to find out about sailboats, gliders, or windmills.

A Visit a working windmill and find out how it works.

Water Power

Paddle Wheels

You Will Need:
- an empty Styrofoam spool
- a plastic jug
- scissors
- a pencil
- a knife
- water
- OR use Tinkertoys for your paddle wheel

What To Do:

1. Mark four paddle shapes on a piece of plastic jug. The shapes should be three inches on the sides, one inch on the bottom, and two inches at the top. Cut out the paddles.

2. *A* Have a grown-up use a knife to cut four slits in the Styrofoam spool. The slits should go up and down on the spool and should be equal distance from each other.

3. Stick the smaller end of a paddle into one of the slits. Do the same with the other paddles. Put the pencil through the middle of the spool.

4. Hold both ends of the pencil. Have a friend pour some water from a cup over the paddles (outdoors or in the sink or bathtub). Watch the water power turn the wheel.

Storm Watch

You Will Need:

- a rainstorm   • a window   • boots and rain gear

What To Do:

1. Watch from a window how a storm grows and changes before, during, and after the rain and wind. Watch the sky, the trees, and the water from the storm.

2. Take a walk after the storm. Wear your rain gear! Notice puddles, streams of water where there usually are none, fallen twigs and branches, flooded areas, and any other things that are different because of the storm.

Waves

You Will Need:

- a tub of water
- some things that float
- a small stone

What To Do:

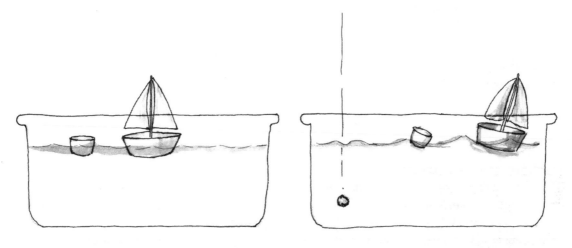

1. Gently put one or more things that float in the tub of water.

2. When the water is still, drop a stone into the tub. Watch the wave power move the floating objects.

Let's Talk About It:

How does water move things?

Did you notice differences between the power of a little water (drops and trickles) and lots of water? How is the wave power different from the power from falling water or the power of rain? What other kinds of water power are there?

During a storm can you tell the difference between water power and wind power? How do they work together?

How can too much water cause problems for people? How can it be scary? How can too little water cause problems for people? How is water helpful? How is it a renewable source of energy?

Other Things To Do:

A Take a trip to a large lake or ocean with a beach to watch how waves work. Watch them carry things to shore and carry sand back to the water.

A Visit a waterfall and follow a stick or other object with your eyes as it is carried by the flow of the water down the falls. Look at the rocks at the bottom of the waterfall. What has the water power done to them?

O Visit a dam or mill wheel at work to see how water power can be used.

Learn safety rules for storms and floods where you live.

2
Seasonal Fun

Background information:

A common characteristic among peacemakers is the tendency to draw boundaries that are highly inclusive. Many peacemakers consider the world their home and all living things as a part of their family. Caring for the world and caring for other people are part of the same process. Learning to care for plants and animals can be especially important for young children because they spend so much of their lives being cared for by others. Becoming nurturant with nature by completing some of the seasonal projects included here allows them the experience of being needed and being able to make a difference for something that needs their care.

Seasonal projects are common activities with young children. They are convenient, timely, and allow children to begin to build an understanding of nature and life cycles. The activities outlined here go a step farther by including an emphasis on cooperation, environmental responsibility, and peacefulness. They stress the importance and benefits of being observant, non-obtrusive, and a part of nature and its seasons. They do not emphasize one season over another. It is hoped that children will be taken outside to experience all seasons with all of their senses.

Some readers may be in climates where a spring/summer/fall/winter progression is not clearly observable. It is hoped that children in such climates will be given the skills to recognize the cycles that do occur in their area, and perhaps will be introduced to the seasons that occur in other places. The activities in this chapter could be altered or could inspire ideas that may be more appropriate for a given climate.

Objectives

For Young Children:
- To learn to recognize and name the four seasons, or seasons that are appropriate in their geographic area.
- To identify what they like and do not like about each season.
- To describe some of the activities of plant and animal life in their region during each of the seasons.
- To plant seeds and watch them grow.

For Early Elementary Children:
- To describe the events of the seasons and to use art, writing, or drama to express feelings about them.
- To identify activities that can be helpful to wildlife during different seasons.
- To help to plan an event appropriate to the seasons.
- To help to care for a garden.

For Later Elementary Children:
- To describe the life cycle of some plants and animals through the seasons.
- To take some responsibility for assisting animals in seasonally appropriate ways.
- To share a celebration of the seasons with others.
- To plan and care for a garden.

For All Children:
- To experience all seasons with all senses.
- To celebrate the characteristics of the seasons with games, food, and fun that are cooperative, environmentally responsible, and peaceful (but not necessarily quiet!).

Spring

Plant a Children's Garden

You Will Need:
- vegetable seeds or small plants   • shovel or trowel   • water and sunshine
- mulch (old leaves, grass trimmings, ashes, or compost from a
  compost jar or from a mulch or compost pile)

What To Do:

1. Decide what you want to plant. Tomatoes, beans, zucchini, or lettuce are not hard to grow. Find out when the best time is to plant those foods in your part of the country. Then, at the right time, find a place for your garden. It can be small or large. There should be lots of sun and good dirt.

2. Mix up the dirt with some mulch or compost to add "food" to the soil. If it is not good soil, mix in some topsoil, too. (You can buy that at a plant store.) Then plant your seeds or plants.

3. Water the plants. Pull weeds carefully around the plants.

4. Pick the vegetables when they are ripe, delicious, and ready to eat in spring, summer, or fall!

Let's Talk About It:

What would happen if you could not get water for your garden? What would happen if there were not enough sun or if the soil were not good?

Where does the food come from that you eat? Where do grocery stores get the food? Do you think you could grow all of the food your family needs? How would it feel to work very hard at growing food for other people and not get paid very much money to support your family?

Decorate a Tree

You Will Need:
• scrap pieces of string or yarn

What To Do:
1. Save small pieces of string or yarn. You can do this throughout the year.

2. When it starts to get warm in the spring, you can help the birds. They need twigs, yarn, and string to build nests for their babies. Decorate a bush or low tree with the string and yarn you saved. Make it easy for the birds to reach.

Wildflower Walk

You Will Need:
- a wild area
- paper and crayons, markers, or paint
- a book about wildflowers (if you want)
- large paper bag

What To Do:

1. Find a wild area for your walk. Make sure there are some wildflowers there. It could be a meadow, a park, a ravine, or a roadside.

2. Take a walk. Watch carefully for wildflowers. When you see one, look at it closely. Look at the colors, shape, number of petals, and type of leaves. Leave wildflowers growing for other people to find and enjoy.

3. Draw a picture of the flower. It is easiest if you take your paper and crayons or markers along on the walk. If you want, look up the name of the flower in a book and label your picture.

4. Mount your pictures on big pieces of brown paper from paper bags and give them to your friends as spring gifts.

Let's Talk About Spring:

What are some ways you can enjoy flowers and plants without picking them? What is the difference between wildflowers and flowers that are not wild? Which do you like better? Why?

Why do wildflowers and other plants grow in spring? What other things grow in spring? What happens to them in the winter?

What things can you learn from watching animals and birds? Think about how they move and how they work.

What changes do you notice as things grow in spring? Why do you think those changes happen? How does spring make you feel? How does it feel to get outside in the spring?

Other Things To Do In Spring:

Go for a walk around your house, school, block, or neighborhood. Collect any litter you see and put it in bags. Save materials to be recycled and pitch the trash into the trash can. Then take a walk and watch for signs of spring like buds, birds, green grass, and weather changes. Tell or write a story about spring things.

Visit baby animals or have some come to visit at your school or church. Watch for baby birds or rabbits in your yard. Talk softly, walk slowly, and be careful not to disturb them.

Have an early spring picnic on the first nice day after winter. Or have a picnic when the first garden food comes up in the spring. Some ideas are onion pizza, rhubarb pie, or a salad with the first greens from your garden. Have a tasting party with your first tender garden veggies.

Give a bag of your finest vegetables to a local soup kitchen that will give meals to people who need them.

Pretend you are a bulb or a seed. Show what the bulb or seed is doing in the winter and then what happens in the spring. Talk about how it might feel to be a new spring flower.

Summer

Backyard Camping

You Will Need:
- a large, old sheet or a blanket   OR   • a tent   • camping stuff
  and a rope or a table

What To Do:
1. You might want to pack up some of the following things for your "camping stuff":

- blanket and pillow
- books or games
- snack or picnic
- canteen or plastic
    container for drink
- flashlight
- camping mat (see
    following activity)

2. Set up your tent in your backyard. You can make one by hanging a sheet or blanket over a rope. OR Use a cardtable or picnic table with a blanket over it. OR Use a real tent if you have one. Pretend you are camping in the woods.

3. *A* After you have practiced at home, go on an overnight camping trip to a state or national park or forest. Help out with the things that need to be done for the trip. Setting up camp, fixing the food, cleaning up, and taking down camp are some things you may be able to do to help.

O Camping Mat

You Will Need:

- 8 large sheets of newspaper
- a sheet of plastic or a garbage bag (2 pieces at least 15″ × 15″)
- heavy tape
- nature things or pictures for decoration
- clear contact paper

What To Do:

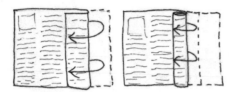

1. Lay a sheet of newspaper out flat. Bring the long sides together in the middle and fold the paper. Then do the same thing another time. Now fold it over so that you have thick strips of paper 3½ inches wide. Do the same thing with all of the sheets of newspaper.

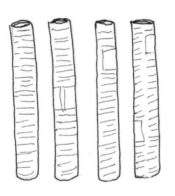  

2. Lay four strips side by side.

3. Weave in the other four strips, one at a time.

4. Tuck in the ends.

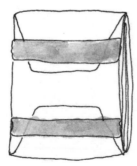 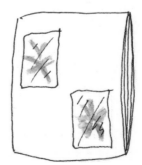

5. You can waterproof your mat. Cover it with plastic or a garbage bag. Tape the ends with heavy tape.

6. Decorate your mat with flat nature objects, drawings, or pictures you have cut out. Cover each object or picture with clear contact paper to keep them waterproof, too.

Summer Snacks

What To Do:

1. Snow Cones. *A* Crush ice in the blender. Pour juice concentrate over it.

2. Homemade Popsicles. Pour juice or pudding into popsicle holders or an ice cube tray. Put sticks or plastic spoons in the middle. Freeze them.

3. "Good Pop." Mix carbonated water and any kind of fruit juice.

4. Ice Cream in a Can. Find a one-pound and a three-pound coffee can. Both should have tight lids. Fill the small can two-thirds full of homemade ice cream mix and put on the lid. Put

the small can in the large can and pack ice between them. Sprinkle some salt on the ice. Put the lid on the large can and roll back and forth between two people. Keep rolling until it is ice cream. You might need to stop and scrape off the sides of the can or add more ice and salt. The time will go quickly if you play a record or sing songs as you roll the can.

Simple homemade ice cream recipe: 1 can (14 oz.) sweetened condensed milk (chilled), 1¾ cup milk, 2 teaspoons vanilla or other flavoring.

5. Fresh fruit and vegetables. Cut up apples, carrots, celery, mushrooms, broccoli, cauliflower, tomatoes, strawberries, pears, plums, or any other fresh fruits and vegetables that you like. Eat them plain or with dip made with plain yogurt and your favorite flavorings.

Let's Talk About Summer:

How does summer make you feel? Do you feel peaceful sometimes? What makes you feel that way? Does the summer heat make you feel tired and restless sometimes? What helps you feel better? Can you think of something that might help others feel better when they're hot and tired?

Why are the "summer snacks" good summer foods?

What are some good things to do when school is out? How can you keep learning in the summertime?

Other Things To Do In Summer:

Take a creek walk. As you walk through the creek, look for signs of wildlife like creek critters and plant life and collect some interesting stones or rocks. You might want to collect some critters in a bucket of creek water. Watch them, and then set them free again.

Set up a "car wash" with water, brushes, sponges, towels, or rags. Drive up your bikes and scrub them clean. Rinse and dry them. Make free coupons for friends and neighbors to have their vehicles cleaned, too. Leave your towels and sponges out to dry in the sun—a solar clothes dryer!

Have a beach party. Set up your "beach." Hide sea shells in some sand, lay out towels, and have tubs or a pool of water for your ocean. Play a record or tape of ocean noises to add to the effect. Beach and ocean pictures mounted here and there could be fun, too. Make a magnet fishing game. Tie a magnet at one end of a string. Tie the other end to a stick or a pole. Make paper fish and attach a paper clip to each one. See if you can catch a fish! Serve "Summer Snacks."

Fall

Harvest Festival

You Will Need:
- records or tapes of dance music
- doughnuts
- string
- apples
- a big bowl or basin of water
- burlap or large paper sacks
- fall decorations
- fall snacks
- friends

What To Do:
1. Plan a harvest festival. Include decorations, games, and snacks (see recipes for special fall foods on following pages) that celebrate fall and the harvest.

2. Decorate for your party. You might want to use fall leaves or corn stalks, gourds, and pumpkins from your garden. You could use window pictures, too. (See the next activity.)

3. Get some simple square or folk dance records for kids or make up your own dances to music.

4. "Bob" for doughnuts. Tie a string around a doughnut. Have someone dangle it in the air. Put your hands behind your back and try to eat the doughnut. Then give someone else a turn.

5. *A* Bob for apples. Fill a tub or basin with water and put one or more apples in it. Put your hands behind your back. Each child should try to grab an apple with his or her teeth. (Use only a little water for young children.)

6. Have sack races. Two children run side by side with their inside feet in a paper or burlap bag together. Or each child hops in his or her own bag. Everyone who finishes wins!

7. Have an old-fashioned "bee." Make a party out of work that needs to be done. This could be husking popcorn, making apple butter, raking leaves, or some other fall task. Be sure to include music, food, and fun!

Let's Talk About It:
What reasons do you have for celebrating fall?

In what ways are dancing and sack races cooperative games? What about bobbing for apples or doughnuts?

Window Pictures

You Will Need:
- wax paper   • leaf collection
-          • iron

What To Do:

1. Arrange a few beautiful leaves between two pieces of wax paper.

2. *A* Iron the whole paper.

3. To make a different picture, use a grater to make little pieces out of old crayons. Sprinkle them on the wax paper alone or with the fall leaves to make a colorful picture.

4. You can cut out some colored paper or part of a paper bag to make a frame for your picture. Then tape it to a window. Or use it as a placemat for your "Harvest Festival."

Let's Talk About Fall:

What kinds of colors, sounds, and smells do you find in fall? What other things are different from other seasons? Does it make you feel sad sometimes to see the plants and flowers die? What other things die? Which will grow again?

Many people burn leaves in the fall. What else can be done with leaves? How could they help your garden?

Fall is the end of the growing season, but it is the beginning of other seasons. What can you think of that starts in the fall?

Other Things To Do In Fall:

Have fun with leaves. Make a leaf collection of beautiful fall colors. Include leaves of different shapes and sizes. When you rake leaves, make a big pile for jumping into or throwing. Or make them into houses with paths for halls and doorways. Use the leaves for composting or pile them or bag them for leaf collection.

Have a fall scavenger hunt. Make a list of nature items you think you could find in your yard or neighborhood. Collect as many of the items as you can. You can work cooperatively in teams. See if all the teams together can find everything. Have each team share their most unusual items.

Plan a Harvest Festival for a group of younger children, a nursing or retirement home, or another group that might enjoy it.

Cook special fall foods.

1) *A* Squash Pie (Crustless)

In a blender put:	1½ cup cooked acorn or butternut squash	
(or mash all	or pumpkin (Butternut is best!)	
ingredients	½ cup honey	
together with a	2 eggs	
potato masher)	1 teaspoon cinnamon	½ teaspoon salt (opt.)
	¼ teaspoon ginger	⅛ teaspoon cloves
	½ teaspoon nutmeg	

Put in a greased 9″ pie pan or 8½″ square pan. Bake at 425 for 15 minutes, then turn the oven down to 350 for 35 to 45 minutes more.

2) *A* Applesauce. Cook apple halves until they are very soft. Run them through a food mill or colander. Or core and peel apples first, cook them until they are soft, and use a potato masher to make applesauce.

3) *A* Crockpot Applebutter

1. Cook for 12 to 14 hours in a covered crockpot:
   12–14 unpeeled apples and 2 cups cider, apple juice, or water

2. Puree the cooked mixture in a blender or food mill.
3. Return the mixture to the crockpot and add:

2 cups sugar	1 teaspoon cinnamon
¼ teaspoon cloves	½ teaspoon nutmeg
¼ teaspoon allspice	

(If you do not have cloves, nutmeg, or allspice, it is okay.)

4. Cook, covered, for 24 to 36 hours.

5. Refrigerate, freeze, or put in sealed jars.

4) *A* Crockpot Peach or Apricot Butter. Wash, peel, and pit fruit, and cook until soft. Add ½ to ¾ cup of sugar to each cup of fruit. Add cinnamon or cloves. Cover and cook on high setting of crockpot for 8-10 hours. Remove cover during last half of cooking. Stir occasionally. (If you use canned fruit, put it in the blender and use less sugar.)

5) Add a pinch of cinnamon to warmed cider.

Winter

Blizzard Bash

You Will Need:

- snow
- sleds or pieces of plastic
- a winter day

What To Do:

1. Sled Run. Take sleds or pieces of plastic to a safe sledding hill or make your own "mini-mountain" by piling up snow.

2. Winter sounds. Listen to the quiet of new snow, the crunch of icy snow, cracking ice, and the sound of winter animals. Enjoy the sounds of your winter fun!

3. Snow Sculptures. Think about what shapes you would like to make with wet snow. Think about what parts you need for your snow sculpture. Different people can make the parts to put together. Use spoons for carving. Sticks and branches can make good decorations. You can use food colors or powdered paint to color the snow.

4. Snow Houses. Make a house out of snow. It can be a place to hide, to stay out of the wind, or to pretend to live. Your can make low walls with carefully placed snow "bricks."

5. If there is no snow, take a winter walk. See how trees, gardens, and yards look in winter. See what colors you can find. Look at the sky and rivers and ponds.

6. Make winter snacks.
    *Pour juice or pudding into popsicle molds, an ice cube tray. or paper cups. Put sticks or plastic spoons in the middle. Cover and freeze the popsicles outside on a very cold day.
    *Make hot chocolate or spiced cider when you come in out of the cold.
    *Make popcorn granola. (See recipe in following activity.)

7. Winter Warm-Ups. Put on some music and have a dance or do stretching and bouncing exercises to warm up.

8. Living Room Obstacle Course. Move furniture and pillows around in your living room so that you can go over, around, between, out, and in things. Play follow the leader, or see how quickly you can finish the obstacle course. Be careful not to break anything!

A Popcorn Granola

You Will Need:
- margarine   • honey   • vanilla   • popcorn and/or cereal
- cinnamon   • cookie sheet   • *A* oven

What To Do:

1. *A* Preheat the oven to 275°. Lightly butter an 11″ × 15″ cookie sheet.

2. Melt together: 1 stick margarine
                    1 cup honey
                    1 teaspoon vanilla

3. Toss together: 1 popper full of popcorn (about 4 cups)
                    2 cups of wheat, rice, or corn cereal squares
                    2 cups of wheat biscuit cereal
                    2 cups of oat circle cereal
                    2 tablespoons of cinnamon

You could use more cereal instead of popcorn, or use any other type of low- or no-sugar cereal instead of the suggestions.

4. Add the liquids to the cereal and popcorn mix and toss again. Spread it on the cookie sheet. *A* Bake it for 40 minutes, stirring every 10 minutes.

5. You also could add coconut, sunflower seeds, or nuts before baking, or raisins or other dried fruit after baking.

   (Note: Please be careful giving very young children popcorn. You may want to use only cereal for them.)

Animal Friends

You Will Need:
- leftover rolls, pretzels, or pieces of bread
- paper and pencil or crayons
- a library

What To Do:

1. Save your leftover rolls, pretzels, and pieces of bread. Spread shortening on them and sprinkle them with bird seed. Decorate a tree or bush with your "ornaments."

2. Learn about animals in the winter. Learn about where they live, what they eat, and what they do to stay warm. You can find the answers in library books or ask someone who knows about animals, or watch the animals and birds yourself.

3. Draw pictures or keep a journal of the winter activities of your animal friends.

Let's Talk About Winter:

What is fun about winter? What is not fun? Does everybody like winter? Why or why not?

How are animals different from people in the way they live in winter? What are some things we can do to help others during the cold winter months?

How can winter be dangerous? What can you do to make it safer for your family and other families?

Other Things To Do In Winter:

Plan an indoor picnic for a wintry day. Spread out an old sheet and invite your friends or family to come. Make lunches for each other and include cheerful notes or pictures with the food. You may want to draw trees to cut out and tape on the wall. Or make a palm tree and add some shells and ocean pictures to your decorations.

Winter is a good time for baking. It will keep you warm! You might want to think about sharing some of your baked foods with someone in your neighborhood who does not get out much in the winter. After you have made your goodies, plan sometime for a little visit to deliver the freshly baked treats.

Section II
Fun With Toys

3

Anything You Want to Be

Background information:

"Dramatic play" or "pretend play" is what children engage in when they take on adult roles or act out some complex situation. Playing house is one of the most common ways this type of play begins. War play, cowboys and Indians, cops and robbers, and superheroes are also examples of dramatic play, but parents and educators have some concern about children playing these roles because of the values those characters and situations represent and because of some of the side effects.

Dramatic play is important because it gives children an opportunity to try out roles—especially adult roles—in a situation in which they can control the outcomes of their behavior, in which they can be as powerful as they want to be, and in which they can even control time. Playing with other children in this way helps children learn social skills such as turn-taking, communication, leading and following, and planning. War play and other violent pretending games may seem to provide some of the same benefits, but those positive aspects can be overshadowed by some important negative ones. Children who are being superheroes may do some dangerous things and often run roughshod over everyone because of their "super" status. Children playing cowboys and Indians are learning some dangerous stereotypes and may be having fun at the expense of racism and prejudice. Studies and observation have shown that children playing such violent games may find it difficult to cooperate, be kind, and help each other when the game is supposed to be over.

The play ideas included here take the excitement, action, strategy, problem-solving, planning, and creativity of some war play and combine that with cooperation, recognition of the needs and rights of various groups, inclusion of everyone, empathy, and an opportunity to explore adult careers and life styles. In addition, nothing suggested here has to be expensive nor does anything require elaborate toys or kits.

Most of the ideas outlined in this chapter are simply initial suggestions or seeds to be sprouted by the creativity of the children using them. Adults should help children get their creative engines started and then ease back and let the children take the lead. Some children who are accustomed to violent play may need some help at first staying on track, but the children should be able to take charge. Adults should not be afraid to participate, however. Rather than using the phrase, "Go play," try, "May I join you?" instead.

Objectives

For Young Children:
- To list some alternatives to play ideas involving war, violent superheroes, or weapons.
- To discover household items that can be used as props for their chosen play ideas.
- To cooperate with other children in acting out roles.

For Early Elementary Children:
- To choose a play idea and follow through with appropriate preparations.
- To define some of the advantages of cooperative, peaceful play.
- To begin to solve problems such as creating props, costumes, and scenery for play.

For Later Elementary Children:
- To plan and carry out an idea for play.
- To explore career options and life styles of some adults.
- To cooperate and show empathy in their play.
- To go beyond traditional play to the actual carrying out of some activities related to the play idea.

For All Children:
- To distinguish between cooperative play and violent play.
- To explore some ways to respond to friends who suggest violent play ideas.
- To practice social skills and communication in a fun, nonthreatening environment.

You can pretend to be anything you want to be! This chapter describes ways kids can play that are not playing war or playing with weapons. There are some ideas here, but you can imagine lots more! These ideas can be more exciting than war play and they are creative instead of destructive. You can "play peace" instead of playing war.

You Will Need:
- props—ideas are given with each activity

What To Do:
1. Gather your friends. (You can do this before or after you choose what to play and get it organized.)

2. Think of what you want to be.

3. Organize your play.
   *Do some "research," like talking to people, reading books, finding pictures, or watching people.
   *Decide what parts there are to play or what characters you will need. Choose which part you want to be, and have your friends choose, too. (You can take turns.) Talk about what the characters do.
   *Find props and add more as you go along.

Firefighters

Props:
- pieces of hoses (or a real, working hose on hot summer days)
- boxes and/or boards
- fire hats (or wear a baseball cap backwards)
- oversized boots and large jackets or raincoats

Things To Be And Do:
Make a firetruck with boxes. Add a bell or ladder to the side. Use your voices for the siren and horn.

Be the firefighters, firetruck drivers, or people in distress.

Be newsreporters covering the fire.

Be forest rangers and animals or people in a forest fire.

O Firehouse Drama

Make up a drama, play, or opera with a firefighting theme. You might want to act out feelings of the people involved. Make one or more backdrops to draw scenery and show where the play is happening. (Sometimes you can get the ends of rolls of newsprint from newspaper offices to use for big backdrops.) You may want to use music or sounds from a tape or record you have bought or made yourself.

Let's Talk About It:

How do firefighters help people? What is dangerous about the job? Why do you think someone might become a firefighter?

Are you afraid of fires sometimes? Is it good to be afraid? When is it a problem to be afraid? Does playing firefighters help?

What things can you and your friends do to help prevent fires in your home? In your school or church? In the forest?

Other Things To Do:

Visit a fire station and ask questions about what the firefighters do and what tools they use. Think of things you can add to your prop collection to make it more complete.

Learn about fire safety at the Red Cross, from the fire marshal, or somewhere else. Learn about "Stop, drop, and roll," and "Hang and drop." Include these safety tips when you play.

If there has been a fire in your community or neighborhood recently, think of ways you can help. Maybe you could collect clothing or toys for the family.

Emergency Medical Team

Props:
- boxes and boards
- blankets
- empty pill bottles
- torn sheets (can be ripped into strips for bandages)
- tubes or straws for IV tubes
- old sheet or blanket and dowels (about 30 inches) for a doll stretcher
- things left over from a hospital or doctor's office (make sure they are clean and safe)
- dolls
- paper and pencils and a clipboard

What To Be And Do:
Make an ambulance with the boxes and boards. Put a red cross on the side. (That means medical help.) Make a hospital emergency room with other boxes and boards and blankets.

Your dolls can be patients or you can work on each other. Be very careful not to hurt your friends. Besides patients, other things you can be are nurses, x-ray and other technicians, doctors, physician's assistants, ambulance drivers, or receptionists (to welcome people, answer phones, write things on forms, and so on).

O First-Hand First Aid

Set up role plays of emergency medical situations. Learn first aid skills from a qualified adult and practice the ones that are safe to practice. Use supplies that can be found easily in an emergency. Use blankets, torn sheets for bandages, rolled newspapers for splints, and so on.

Let's Talk About It:
Doctors, nurses, technicians, and the others are called a medical team. Why do they have to work together? How are their jobs different? How is a medical team like a baseball team? How is it different?

How does it feel to be sick or hurt? What helps you feel better? How can you do those things for someone else? What feels good about helping people who are hurt? What feels sad?

Other Things To Do:
A Visit a doctor's office or hospital. Ask the different medical people what jobs they do, and what equipment they need to do their jobs.

Talk to someone from the children's ward in a hospital near you. Find out if you can help. Making cards, collecting toys, or making simple games are some things you might be able to do to help.

Community Workers

Office Workers

Props:
- "junk mail"—forms, papers, stamps (maybe used ones, Easter or Christmas Seals, or magazine subscription stamps), computer paper, and envelopes from home or an office
- table and chair or boxes for a desk
- pencils or pens
- a can for a pencil holder
- carbon paper scraps to make copies of what you write
- telephones (old ones, play ones, or two cans or paper cups with strings strung through the bottom)
- old rubber stamps and an ink pad
- box for a file drawer and used file folders
- old typewriter or a homemade computer (shoe box or an upside-down egg carton for a keyboard and a box for a monitor)

What To Do And Be:

Decide what kind of office you want to make. You could write things, sell things, buy things, solve problems, or something else. Decide if people come in to see you in your office and, if they do, what they do while they are there.

You can be secretaries, receptionists, the "boss" (take turns!), reporters, sales people, accountants (people who take care of money), custodians (people who clean up), or computer programmers.

Type letters and mail them. Make phone calls. Sort things in file folders. Do not forget to take your coffee break!

O Kids' Press
(Younger children can do this with help.)

Set up your own newspaper office. It could be in a corner of your classroom, playroom, or bedroom. Get a good supply of paper (Use recycled paper if you can!), pens, pencils, and a typewriter or a computer (if you have one). Everyone can contribute! You could use drawings, stories, news articles, photographs, weather, recipes, book and movie reviews, sports, and interviews. Make copies of your paper and give them away or sell them to pay for printing costs.

Let's Talk About It:

What kinds of offices have you seen? What other kinds of offices are there?

What do office workers need to know how to do? How do you think office work is different now than it used to be many years ago? How do people in offices help others?

How does it feel to be the boss? How does it feel to listen to the boss? What are some good ways to act when you are the boss and what are some ways that are not helpful? How can you make decisions with your "co-workers?"

Other Things To Do:
　　A Visit the office in your school or church or other place in your community. Ask about the equipment they have and how it is used.

　　Try out different kinds of offices in your play.

Store

Props:
- coupons
- sales receipts
- paper bags
- play money (you can make some with paper and pencils)
- boxes and boards to set up the store
- a box and egg carton to make a cash register
- store items:
    - Grocery store—empty food boxes and cans (ask your mom or dad to open them from the bottom so they will look full), egg cartons, milk jugs, and other containers.
    - Other stores—clothing, shoes, art work, or whatever is needed for different kinds of stores.

What To Do And Be:
Sort out the items and set up your store. Think of ways to help people know what is for sale, how to find it, and how much it costs.

Some people can be store workers and some can be customers. Then you can switch.

O Trading Post

Set up a trading post with "treasures" that you would not mind trading away for something else. (Be sure to get permission from your parents, and make sure you do not trade away something that is not yours!) Your friends can each have a section of the trading post for their treasures. You could make trading coupons. You might want to trade small toys, baseball cards, stickers, books, jewelry, or other things. Before you trade, both people need to be satisfied with what they are giving and what they are getting.

Let's Talk About It:
What kinds of things happen in stores that you could include in your play? How do people pay for things they buy (cash, checks, credit, food stamps, trades)? How do people get the things they need if they do not go to stores?

Where do stores get the things they sell? What do the stores need money for besides buying things to sell?

Other Things To Do:
Set up a shopping mall with different kinds of stores (grocery, art store, pet store, book store, ice cream shop, clothing store), a bank, a restaurant, a movie theater, and anything else you can think of.

A Visit a "resale" store that sells used clothing, furniture, books, or cars. Ask how they get the things they sell. Find out how it is different from stores that sell new things.

A Visit a food bank or a place that gives away used clothing, toys, or furniture. Find out how that type of "store" is different from a place that sells things. Collect food items or old clothing, toys, or furniture to give to the food bank or distribution center.

Set up a lemonade stand with your friends. Offer the refreshments free or donate the money to a good cause.

Other Workers

1. Factory Workers. You could set up a clothing factory using paper bags and tape for making vests, moccasins, and handbags.

2. Musicians. Gather instruments around your house or school, or make your own. You could make maracas with beans in a container with a lid; a kazoo out of wax paper over a comb, or put wax paper over the end of a paper towel roll and hold it with a rubber band; cymbals from a pan lid with wooden spoon; or a guitar out of rubber bands stretched across a box. Think of other instruments, too.

3. Transportation Workers. Use boxes, chairs, boards, and other props to make trains, buses, trucks, planes, and other vehicles.

4. Librarians. Gather books and cards for your library. You can set up your own library story hour or reading program.

O Other Job Ideas

Set up a restaurant for your family or friends. Give out menus and free coupons for meals. With some help from a grown-up you can plan the menu, fix the food, serve it, and clean up afterwards.

A Set up a carpentry shop to make things for your friends. Get some used or scrap wood. You could make toys, tree houses for bird friends, or any other ideas you might have. Be sure to have grown-ups close by if you use real tools, so that they can show you safety tips.

Let's Talk About It:

What kinds of jobs would you enjoy doing? Why?

Why do you think people go to work? What kinds of jobs do you think are most interesting? What jobs are really important for people to do? Why do you think so?

Other Things To Do:

When you go places in your community, watch people doing different kinds of jobs. See how many different jobs you notice people doing. Talk to people. Ask them what they like best about their jobs. Ask them what they do not like about their jobs.

Talk to people in a union about their jobs and what it is like to belong to a union.

A Have a Neighborhood Scavenger Hunt. Collect business cards and ads or flyers from different businesses and services in your neighborhood. See how many you and your friends can collect.

Space Explorers

Props:

- boxes, cardboard tubes, and paint to make a spaceship
- ice cream buckets with a rectangle cut out or large plastic bowls for space helmets.
- rocks for "moon rocks," and/ or blankets for other planetary surfaces
- "camera" and other equipment
- space snacks—dried fruit or fruit leather

What To Do And Be:

Make your spaceship. Make the planet or moon that you will visit.

You can have a ship captain (take turns!), navigator, medical person, communications expert, friendly aliens, and whatever else you want.

**O* Space Models*

Make your own spaceship models using cardboard, tin foil, aluminum cans, and other simple materials. Or make a galaxy mobile of planets, stars, suns, and moons.

Let's Talk About It:

What kinds of space stories do you like best? Why? Who are the characters? What are they like? What kinds of places would you like to explore if you could go up into space? What would you expect to find?

Other Things To Do:

Read science fiction books or watch some science fiction shows. Think about how "aliens" are described in the books or shows. Decide whether they are interesting and helpful or bad and scary. Talk about why they are pictured the way they are. Write your own science fiction stories and create models or star maps to go with them. Be sure to include helpful aliens.

A Visit a museum with a space exhibit. Learn about the planets, stars, and galaxies to help with your story writing.

O Learn about earth's space exploration programs. Find out about peaceful uses of outer space and why it is important to keep outer space from becoming a war zone.

Make a space mural with paper and crayons and glitter or tin foil stars.

Deserted Tropical Island

Props:
- homemade clothes (from paper bags) or torn clothes (ask Dad to check his t-shirt drawer)
- long sticks or branches (Be careful with these! Younger children will need help.)
- blankets or sheets
- pots and pans
- buckets, rope, compass, notebook and pencil, and whatever else you think you might find aboard a wrecked ship
- paper and/or cardboard to make palm trees, balls wrapped with brown paper to make coconuts
- fruit and nuts or coconut for a tropical snack

What To Do And Be:

Imagine being shipwrecked on an island where no other people live. Build your shelter and other things you will need to survive. Think about how you will get water, communicate, and entertain yourselves.

Be a family, a group of friends, or the workers and passengers from the ship that was wrecked.

O Diorama

Make a model of a desert island using a cardboard box with only a bottom and two sides. You can use clay or salt dough for modeling. You also can use sand, rocks, tin foil, colored paper, and other nature objects or art supplies. Make caves, trees, the seashore, waterfalls, or whatever else you think would be on a desert island. You could read *Swiss Family Robinson* to get some ideas.

- Salt Dough: Mix 2 cups flour, 1 cup water, and 1 cup salt.

Let's Talk About It:

How do you think it would feel to live on a deserted island? How would it feel not to have electricity or running water or TV? What would you miss the most? What would be good about it?

How would it feel to be with the same small group of people all of the time? Would you get lonely sometimes? Do you think it would be hard to get along sometimes?

Other Things To Do:

Talk to senior citizens about what life used to be like before modern luxuries. Ask them what stories they remember about their parents and grandparents back in the days before cars, TV, electricity, and other modern inventions.

Mystery Solvers

Props:
- paper and pencil to write coded messages
- lemon juice, cotton swabs, and a toaster (*O*) for invisible ink messages
- magnifying glass and flashlight
- flour for fingerprints
- a mystery to solve!

What To Do And Be:

Make up secret codes with your friends by having symbols or letters or numbers stand for other letters or other information.

Write invisible ink messages using lemon juice and writing with a cotton swab "pen." To read the message, let it dry and lay the paper on top of the toaster (*O*). Set it on a low setting and push the handle down. (Young children should ask an adult to help.) Watch the message appear. Move the paper away and pop the toaster up as soon as you can read the message.

You and your friends could sign your messages with ink or paint fingerprints. Have a master fingerprint file with everyone's fingerprints in it so that you can tell who wrote the message.

Something is missing! Tell your family you will help to find things. You probably will need a flashlight and magnifying glass for these cases. Search everywhere, especially under other things. Find out who saw the item last and try to figure out what happened since then.

O Make a map of your house, school, or neighborhood and mark the places you need to search or places under investigation in a mystery. You could try to give the map to other friends and see if they could follow it to find something or someone.

Hide something. Then set up mystery clues for your friends with fingerprints or footprints made with flour or with cut-out paper footprints. Or in the summer make a trail with water on the sidewalk and driveways. Tell your friends when they are getting "hot" (close to the hidden object) or "cold" (getting farther from the hidden object). Then switch places.

Let's Talk About It:

What is fun about solving mysteries and secret codes? Can using secret codes make people feel bad sometimes? How?

Can you think of other ideas for solving mysteries?

Can solving a mystery ever help to avoid an argument?

Other Things To Do:

Read mystery books to get more play ideas.

Make a treasure hunt. Half of the group could set up a treasure hunt for the other half. Use clues with pictures or words, or make a treasure map.

When you see two people having an argument, see if there is a mystery that you could help to solve. Maybe the mystery is finding out what really happened to someone or something or finding missing valuables. Or maybe the mystery is finding a new way to look at the situation or solve the problem. Maybe you could help to stop the argument!

Dragons and Unicorns

Props:
- costumes: scarves, long skirts, tights, t-shirts with ties around the waist, hats made from newspaper or paper bags
- boxes and boards
- "candles" made from rolled up paper, colored or painted at the top
- a fireplace made in a box turned on its side with sticks or logs inside and crumpled red, orange, and blue paper to make the fire
- plates and cups, beds, and chairs; real or pretend
- an area for your cottage or castle

What To Do And Be:

Make a papier-mache creature—maybe a dragon or unicorn—for your story. You can use balloons, boxes, bags (blow air into a bag and tie it), other containers, chicken wire, and lots of tape to make your shape. Then cover it with papier-mache.

Papier-Mache

Tear lots of newspaper strips.

Soak the strips in either liquid starch or a mixture of flour and water.

Cover your shape with the strips, one layer at a time.

This is a great cooperative project, especially if your creature is large!

Make up a story using your creature, the costumes you made, and whatever other props you need.

Let's Talk About It:

What are your favorite fairy tales? Why?

What are the people like in fairy tales? Who are the "bad" guys? Do they have a chance to get better or to do good things? Who are the "good" guys? Are they supposed to be rich at the beginning or become rich in the story? Is that fair? Are girls and women as smart and important as the boys and men? Can you make up your own fairy tale that is fair for everyone?

Other Things To Do:

Read lots of fairy tales from different times and different countries. Think about the good guys and the bad guys, the men and women, and how the people change.

Make one of your dragon and unicorn stories into a play to act out for other people. Practice the play. You can use words or no words. Use music if you like. Decide with your friends which characters you need and what they should do. Remember to include everyone who wants to be in the play. After you have worked on your play, you may want to act it out for someone—maybe your family, your senior citizen friends, or some younger children.

4
Old Toys, New Toys

Background information:

If play is a child's work, toys are the tools of the child's trade. Good toys could be items manufactured for the specific purpose of facilitating certain types of play, or they could be some unlikely objects that children find that inspire their imagination and creativity. The commercial toy market is a fairly recent phenomenon, and its explosion is probably related to the discovery and acceptance of the fact that play is a necessary and important part of children's development. The designing and selling of toys has both positive and negative implications; toys are available that have been carefully structured to be of interest to children of particular ages and to be safe for their play and exploration, yet play also has become expensive and children have become dependent on toys, often very specific toys, for their fun.

One of the most alarming outcomes of the modern commercial toy market is the dominance of violent toys and "action figures." Not only are these heavily marketed on television and in other children's media and displayed in a dominant fashion in stores, but children's television has become a method of providing advertising for these toys in program format. It remains to be seen whether such programs will begin to be regulated again, but children have been effected in any case. They have been given the message that all children should have these toys.

This chapter concentrates on alternatives to war toys and commercialism in the toy market. It helps children explore and identify peaceful ways of using toys and ways to respond to friends who suggest war play. It also helps children use their imagination and creativity to design their own toys to meet their own needs and values. Perhaps children who participate in these activities could begin to change the toy market itself!

Objectives

For Young Children:
- To begin to identify war toys and peace toys.
- To learn that safety is important when dealing with toys.
- To increase their repertoire of play ideas.

For Early Elementary Children:
- to identify some methods of dealing with friends who suggest war play.
- To check some toys for safety.
- To explore the relationship between war toys and fights or arguments among friends.

For Later Elementary Children:
- To communicate their feelings about war toys to others.
- To design unique toys with safety in mind.
- To redirect friends who suggest war play.

For All Children:
- To consider what makes toys fun.
- To recycle throw-aways by making toys.
- To utilize their creativity in designing peaceful toys.
- To become less dependent on commercial toy products to have fun.

Building for Peace

You Will Need:
- blocks or other building toys   • your imagination
- other props as needed

What To Do:
1. Get out some building toys like blocks, Legos, or TinkerToys. Or make your own (see Blocks in the section on homemade toys).

2. Brainstorm with your friends about things you could build. That means you think up lots of ideas. Kids sometimes use toys like these to make guns and war toys, so think about what you could build that would be peaceful.

Some ideas are:

instead of a battlefield,   make a city with offices, factories, stores, restaurants, and homes.

instead of weapons,   make tools to use when you pretend to do different jobs. Try walkie-talkies (cover the blocks with tin foil), hammers for building, and lots of other tools.

instead of guns,   make cameras and shoot pictures instead of bullets.

instead of tanks or fighter planes,   make vehicles like trains, spaceships, or cool cars

instead of a fort,   make a space city or village from a story you like.

3. Think about things you could add to your project as you go along. Your friends can share lots of ideas, too.

Let's Talk About It:
What are some details you can put into your building project? Are there other things from around your house or school that you could add? What other ideas for playing can you think of to try some other time?

How is building for peace different from preparing for "war?"

When you play war or play with violent toys, do you and your friends have arguments and fights? What happens when you play with peace toys? Is it different?

What is fun about playing war? What is not much fun? How does it feel to think up ideas for play that are not war play?

Other Things To Do:

The next time a friend gets the idea to play a war game, suggest one of your other exciting ideas for play.

Try a role play. Pretend someone shoots you with a Lego "gun." What could you do? What else could you do? Role play other situations, too.

When you see some friends having a fight or an argument, try to be a peacemaker (even if you do not call yourself that).

Imagine-a-Toy

You Will Need:

- paper
- crayons or markers
- friends or family

What To Do:

1. Think about a new toy that could be made that would be a peace toy instead of a war toy.

2. Draw an advertisement for your toy. Make it big and colorful so that it would get someone's attention.

3. Share your ads with your friends or family. Tell them what your toy idea was and what would be special about your toy.

Let's Talk About It:

What do you think a "peace toy" would be? How would it be different from other toys?

What would make your toy fun to play with?

Why do you think there are not more peace toys in stores? Why do you think there are so many war toys in stores?

Other Things To Do:

Send your ad to a toy company that makes war toys. Get the address from a war toy package at a store, or ask for the address from the store manager. Tell the toy company what you do not like about war toys and why you think your ideas for peace toys would be better for kids. A grown-up can write the letter for you if you explain what you want to say.

Collect the ads that you and your friends have made. Make a display of ads for peace toys. Put it in a place where many people will see it.

Look at the toy sections of stores in your town or city. What kinds of war toys do they have? Are they in the front or the back of the store? How much room do they take up? Write the managers of stores that sell war toys. Tell them what you think.

If you or your friends have war toys, think about throwing them away to make your house a "War Toy Free Zone." Or think about ways to make the war toys into peace toys. Make rules for friends using war toys at your house. Some rules might be "No shooting people or animals," or "No messing up anything someone else made."

Create-a-Toy

You Will Need:
- empty spools
- film cans
- plastic mesh bags from oranges or onions
- small and large paper bags
- potato chip cans
- canning rings or jar lids
- glue, tape, string as needed
- wood, fabric scraps, paint
- other things that usually are thrown away

What To Do:
1. Collect some things that usually get thrown away. Pick out one or more items from those you collected. Think of three ways you could make the item(s) into a toy.

2. Make at least one of your toy ideas. Try playing with the toy.

3. *A* If your toy is for a young child, ask a grown-up to check if the toy is safe. If it is, give it to a child.

4. Pick another item or two and think of more toy ideas.

Let's Talk About It:
How did your toy work?

Why is it important to check for toy safety?

How did you decide what kinds of toys you could make? What makes your toys fun?

Other Things To Do:
Learn about toy safety. Find out how to check your toys for safety. Learn how to check young children's toys, too.

Homemade Fun

Puppets

You Will Need:

- small paper bags
- plastic spoons
- colored markers
- paper plates or cardboard
- paper
- popsicle sticks or straws
- yarn or fabric scraps
- socks

What To Do:

1. Make different kinds of puppets.

    *Paper bag puppet. When the bag is folded flat, use the folded end as the mouth. You can make the puppet talk if you put your hand inside with your fingers in the flap. Decorate it with eyes, nose, mouth, and hair.

    *Paper plate puppet. Staple, tape, or glue a popsicle stick or straw to a paper plate or to cardboard shaped like a head. Decorate it.

    *Sock puppets. Draw a face on the toe end of an old sock, or glue or sew things on for a face.

    *Tiny puppets. Draw a face on the bowl of a plastic spoon. Or make a paper ring for your finger and draw or glue a face on it. Or make a little face on your finger or thumb.

2. Use your puppets to act out a play or to talk about anything you would like.

Dolls and Dollhouse

You Will Need:
- glue
- clothespins (with round heads)
- a shoe box
- yarn
- little boxes and spools
- crayons or markers
- fabric scraps
- paint and brush
- old wallpaper books from a decorating store (if you want)

What To Do:
1. Make faces on the clothespins. Make hair and clothes out of pieces of material and yarn. Glue them on the clothespins.

2. Make a house for your dolls. Cut out the top and one side of a shoe box. Glue fabric or wallpaper onto the inside of your doll house. Or make your own wallpaper with crayons, paint, or markers on paper. Make furniture with little boxes and spools. You can paint the furniture and house if you like.

Playdough

You Will Need:
- water
- food color
- a stove or microwave oven
- flour
- salt
- vegetable oil
- alum

household items to use with playdough: canning rings, cookie cutters. plastic silverware, popsicle sticks, a food press or mill, a rolling pin or long cylinder blocks, wooden or plastic hammers, safety scissors, plastic spools, and wire screen are some ideas

What To Do:

1. *A* Make the playdough. Mix 2¼ cups flour, ½ cup salt, 3 tablespoons oil, and 1 tablespoon alum. Boil 2 cups of water and add a few drops of food color. Add the boiling water to the flour mixture and stir until smooth. (Note: This playdough will not harden.)

2. Enjoy making different shapes and designs with your playdough.

3. You might want to make beads, mobiles, or ornaments out of playdough. You will need a mixture that gets hard for those things. Mix 2 cups of flour, 1 cup water, and 1 cup salt until smooth. Make your beads, shapes to hang on the mobile, or ornaments. Stick a straw through your shape to make a hole as it dries. Paint the shapes when they are dry, if you like.

Carton Blocks

You Will Need:
- empty milk cartons or other boxes and containers of different sizes
- heavy tape
- contact paper, wallpaper, or other paper and glue, if you want

What To Do:

1. Tape the open end of the milk cartons or boxes so that they look like blocks. Decorate them with contact paper, wallpaper, or other paper and glue, if you want.

2. After you have collected a lot of blocks, you can use them for building. Keep collecting containers. The more you make, the better.

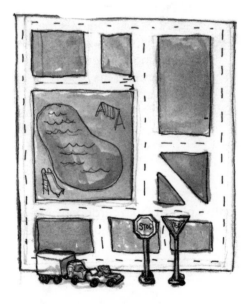

Road Map

You Will Need:
- an old sheet or tablecloth or a large piece of paper
- paints, markers, or crayons
- little cars or blocks (to use as cars)
- blocks and other things to make houses, people, trees, and other scenery

What To Do:

1. Draw roads on a large piece of paper or an old sheet. Make fields or city streets.

2. Use blocks for houses or other buildings. You can make road signs, too. Draw them and cut them out. Then tape them to a straw stuck into a little playdough.

3. Drive your cars on the roads.

Books

You Will Need:
- paper   • photographs or art work
  - cardboard or stiff paper
  - a hole punch and yarn OR
    a stapler
  - fabric scraps
- clear contact paper to cover pages,
  if you want

What To Do:
1. You can write your own book! It can be a story about you or a make-believe story. Think about your story and draw pictures to show what happens. If you want words, you can write them on the pictures, or have a grown-up help you. You also could use real photographs.

2. Make a cover for your book. Staple stiff paper to the front and back and draw a picture on the front. Or make a cardboard cover and decorate it with fabric scraps. You can punch holes in the cover and in the pages and tie them together with yarn.

Puzzles

You Will Need:
- magazines with pictures that you like (they may be pictures of different kinds of people and places around the world)
  - a large catalogue
- wax paper   • thin cardboard
  - glue   • scissors
  - envelopes

What To Do:
1. Look for large magazine pictures. Glue each picture onto a piece of thin cardboard. Make sure it is stuck all over, especially at the corners. Cut off any extra cardboard around the edges of the pictures.

2. Put wax paper on top of and underneath the pictures. Put the pictures between pages of a heavy catalogue or book. Let the glue dry overnight.

3. Take the pictures out of the catalogue. Throw away the wax paper, or save it (if it is not too messy) to use with your next puzzle. Cut the pictures into puzzle piece shapes. Put the pieces of each puzzle in an envelope. Write the name of the puzzle on the outside.

4. Put the puzzles back together. Share the puzzles with your friends.

Collections

You Will Need:
- a box or boxes
- space to store your things

What To Do:

1. Think about some things you might want to collect. Talk to some people your age and other people about what collections they have. Some of the older people in your family or a friend's family might have great collection ideas.

Some ideas are: things from nature like rocks or leaves, things from different places like stamps or napkins, baseball cards, postcards, or just "good stuff" that you want to save for future projects. There are plenty of things you can collect that do not cost much money.

2. Make a system for storing your collection. You might want to sort and organize your collections. Write down the date and place you found each thing or who gave it to you. You can go to the library and find out more about your collections. Tell other people what you are collecting; they might want to find things for you, too. Help your friends with their collections, also!

Let's Talk About It:

What feels good about making your own toys and things for fun? In what ways is it helpful? (Think about money, trash problems, and how much fun toys are.)

What other play ideas can you think of that use things that are already around your house and school?

What do you think when you hear children say they need toys that cost a lot of money? Do you think that is true for you?

Other Things To Do:

Think about other homemade toys you could make. Make a homemade toy gift for a friend or brother or sister.

Make a toy catalogue of all the toys you made.

Go to the library and find books about toys that children played with in the past. See if the books give you ideas for other toys you could make.

Section III
Fun With People

5

Cooperative Game Festival

Background information:

Children in this society are surrounded by competitive games. From professional sports to board games to the Special Olympics there are examples of fun and recreation that are based on winners and losers, overcoming others, and elimination of those who do not measure up. The implications for self-esteem, interpersonal relationships, and enjoyment of leisure time are serious, especially for children. What a tragedy to see the utter despair of an athlete who just came in second in a world-class contest!

Cooperative games are based on three major concepts: success is best achieved by working together; games are based on inclusion of all rather than elimination of some; and they are fun! Many people believe competition with others is the key to excitement and fun in games. While it is true that some attempts at the creation of cooperative games have been lifeless and boring, well-designed games should be fun—for everyone, not just the winners. Challenge should be a part of the activities, and competition with one's own past performance can help to construct the challenge.

It is likely that people always will compare themselves with others, and competitive and comparative sports and games may well have a place in this society. But cooperative play can begin to provide a more balanced exposure and experience for children. This is important especially when social skills and self-esteem are under development.

Several game ideas are presented here. Please note that many more traditional games can be converted to a cooperative model and that children's own imaginations can create many original ones.

Objectives

For Young Children:
- To learn how to play several cooperative games.
- To increase their ability to cooperate with others.

For Early Elementary Children:
- To learn the characteristics of cooperative games.
- To explore the reasons why certain kinds of games are fun.

For Later Elementary Children:
- To convert one or more traditional games to a cooperative format.
- To create one or more original cooperative games.
- To explore their feelings and attitudes toward competitive sports and games.

For All Children:
- To have fun!

Friendly Charades

You Will Need:

- yourself   • your imagination

Animals and Bugs

What To Do:

1. Think about an animal or bug you could be.

2. Pretend to be that animal or bug. Use your body and your voice. Do this with friends to make a zoo, farm, forest, or ocean full of different animals and bugs.

Shapes and Letters

What To Do:

1. Pick a shape or letter. Work with a friend or alone. It might help to draw a picture of the shape or letter first.

2. Make the shape with your body. Try different shapes and letters with your friends.

Popcorn Popper and Other Machines

What To Do:

1. Think about a popcorn popper. Think about what it looks like, what it does, and how it sounds. Think about the different parts.

2. Use your body and voice to make a popcorn popper. Your friends can help.

3. Think about other machines you can make. A clothes washer, toaster, and electric mixer are some ideas to try.

Let's Talk About It:

What is it like to play these games alone? How is it different playing them with a group of children?

Which things were easy to imitate? Which things were harder? Which things could you do alone and which things needed the help of friends?

Other Things To Do:

One person or a group can be a bug, shape, or machine while the others guess what it is.

Take photos of your game.

Think of other things you could pretend to be.

Musical Chairs

You Will Need:
- sturdy chairs—one fewer than the number of people playing
- friends
- music
- a leader

What To Do:

1. Arrange the chairs in a line, a circle, or any other shape.

2. The leader plays the music and everyone walks, marches, or dances around. The leader stops the music at any time.

3. When the music stops, everyone finds a chair. One person will need to share a chair with someone.

4. Take away a chair each time. More and more people will have to share chairs when the music stops.

5. The last time around, everyone will be sharing only one chair.

Let's Talk About It:
What did you do to figure out how to get everyone on one chair?

How does it feel to be playing musical chairs and be out of the game if you do not have a chair? How is this way of playing different?

Other Things To Do:
Use a wind-up music box for the music. Then everyone can play! Or make your own music for the game with singing or instruments. Or have one person ring a bell when it is time to sit down.

Think of your own cooperative ways to play musical chairs. Some ideas: play musical hugs—when the music stops find someone to hug; musical falls—everyone falls to the floor; or musical freeze—everyone freezes when the music stops.

Think of ways to make other party games cooperative. It should be a game that lets everyone win and have fun, everyone works together, and no one is left out.

Recycle an Old Sheet

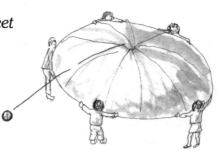

You Will Need:
- an old sheet (if you have a large group, sew four sheets together)
  - friends

What To Do:
1. Lay the sheet out flat. Gather around it.

2. Have each person hold the edge of the sheet. Stand up, kneel down, raise your hands together, lower them together.

3. Try many different games with your "parachute." Some ideas are:
- make mountains, valleys, waves.
- make a popcorn popper by throwing yarn pom-poms, foam balls, or ping pong balls in the middle.
- make a dome to sit under by bringing the parachute down behind your backs.
- raise arms together and let go.
- play balloon volley—with one sheet, or have two groups with sheets hit the balloon back and forth. In the summer use water balloons!

Use your imagination!

Let's Talk About It:
What other things can you imagine with your sheet? What other objects could you use with the sheet?

How does it work? What keeps the sheet up? Does it work better with more or fewer people? What happens when you all do the same thing at the same time? How is it different when you do different things?

Other Things To Do:
A Make your "parachute" even bigger. Sew more sheets together. How does the activity change as your parachute gets bigger? How many more people do you need?

Decorate the sheets.

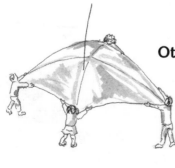

Balloon Volley

You Will Need:
- balloons

What To Do:

1. Throw one balloon up in the air. Keep hitting it to make sure it does not touch the ground.

2. Add more balloons as you go. Remember that everyone has to work together to make sure the balloons stay in the air.

Let's Talk About It:

Can you do this activity with more balloons than people?

Why is this a cooperative game? What other kinds of cooperative games can you play with balloons

Other Things To Do:

Try to think of a game with popping balloons.

Make up other rules for this game. Maybe no one may hit the balloon two times in a row. Maybe people may use only one hand. Or maybe you could try holding hands while you play.

A Try your balloon volley with water balloons in the summer. Expect to get wet!

Play volleyball with or without a net with a giant ball or beach ball. More than one person at a time will have to help hit the ball.

Set up a cooperative game with other types of balls, flying disks, and other sports equipment.

Follow the Leader

You Will Need:
- friends
- a leader
- lots of space inside or out

What To Do:
1. Line up. The person in front starts by being the leader.

2. Each person follows, watches, and does exactly what the person in front does. The leader may use arms, legs, sounds, or whatever.

3. Each person should get a turn to be the leader.

Let's Talk About It:
Did each person get a chance to be the leader?

Why is that important? How does it feel to lead? How does it feel to follow? How would it feel to always lead? How would it feel to always follow?

Other Things To Do:
A Set up an obstacle course with boxes, tires, boards, chairs, and other things. Remember to watch what the leader does!

Play *Follow the Leader* to music.

Crazy Creatures

You Will Need:
- friends
- tape
- paper, crayons, and scissors for everyone

What To Do:

1. Work together to make an animal or creature. Think about all of the parts your creature might have. One person should whisper to each of the other people what part that person should make. Make sure there is a part for each person in the group. People could make a head, a body, legs, arms, eyes, ears, mouth, hands, feet, and maybe a tail or horns or other parts you might think of.

2. You can do this with a few people or a lot. Have each person draw or color the part he or she was asked to make. Then have them cut the part out. If you have just a few people, each person can make more than one part. If you have lots of people, you can work as a team or divide up and make more creatures.

3. Put the creature together when everyone is done. Tape it together on the floor or wall. You probably will have a crazy creature!

Let's Talk About It:

What is fun about working together on something silly like "creature creating?" What other things could you create this way? What parts would you need?

Did each person feel like an important member of the group? Why or why not? How does each person add something special to the creature?

Other Things To Do:

Make other cooperative creatures. Make a very silly one or a very scary one. If you have more than one group, mix up the creatures or add all the parts together. Or make clothes for your creature. Have one person tell each person one piece of clothing to make.

Tell a cooperative story. Have one person start the story and tell a few lines. Then another person should make up the next part. Keep going until each person has had at least one turn or until the story ends.

O Trust Walk

You Will Need:
> • one friend
> • a blindfold (a scarf, handkerchief, or headband)

What To Do:

1. Put the blindfold over your friend's eyes. Or that person should keep his or her eyes closed.

2. Gently take your friend's arm. Lead him or her on a walk. Talk to your friend. Say what you see and where things are so he or she will not bump or fall down. Switch places.

Let's Talk About It:

How did it feel to be the leader? Was it hard to make sure your friend was safe?

How did it feel to not be able to see? Was it scary? Did your friend help you feel better?

How good was your partner at letting you know what to do or what you might run into? Do you think a good communicator is easier to trust in this game than someone who is not so good at talking to you?

Can you imagine how it might feel to not ever be able to see?

Other Things To Do:

O Try a trust walk without any speaking. Just gently lead and touch the other person to let him or her know when to stop or turn or step over something.

A Put blindfolds on several people. Have the people hold hands in a line. One "seeing" person should be at the front giving directions.

Talk with a blind person. Ask how he or she communicates. Learn some things that you can do to use your other senses.

Partner Pictures

You Will Need:
- large pieces of paper
- a partner
- collage materials—fabric, yarn, paper, and so on
- markers or crayons
- glue

What To Do:
1. Lie down on a large piece of paper. Have your partner trace your body.

2. Trade places.

3. Work together to decorate each other's pictures using fabric, yarn, paper, drawings, and so on.

Let's Talk About It:
Could you do this activity alone? Why is it better with a friend?

Did the two of you agree on ideas about how to decorate the pictures? How did you work it out if you did not agree?

How does it feel doing an art activity with another person?

Other Things To Do:
Make shadow pictures of your friend outside on a sunny day.

Try other cooperative art work as festival activities.

Backrub Train

You Will Need:
- fingers   • backs

What To Do:
1. Stand or sit in a circle. Everyone should turn sideways the same direction.

2. Rub the back of the person in front of you.

3. Think happy thoughts about the person whose back you are rubbing.

4. Then turn around and rub another person's back. Relax and enjoy!

Let's Talk About It:
How did it feel to give a rub? How did it feel to get a rub?

Could you relax? Did you like this cooperative game?

Other Things To Do:
Take time out in your day to give a friend or someone in your family a backrub. Everyone needs a chance to relax!

Rub a friend's feet or hands. Use lotion if you want.

Close your eyes and try to find the people around you with your hands. Gently touch their faces to guess who they are.

6

Celebration Ideas

Background information:

Most of the previous chapters in this book have provided specific ideas for fun, play, and exploration. The idea of celebration is a much broader one, however, and here the attempt is to pull many types of smaller activities into a celebration experience. Celebration should be in the heart of any peacemaker as he or she rejoices in signs of peace and justice and looks with hope toward the future.

An important aspect of celebration is its communal nature. Jointly planned social activities are perfect for children at the stages being targeted here. Most of these children are at what has been called the "gang years." These are the years during which children love to do things together. They begin to identify closely with their peers and need their company. At the same time, they continue to need and enjoy adult leadership and companionship. Celebrating together provides children the opportunity to develop social skills, to build self-esteem in themselves and others, and polish planning skills.

This chapter provides a variety of ideas for fun, celebration, and creativity. Ideas are presented that should make it possible for kids to experience many of the benefits of parades, fairs, and festivals without waiting for someone else to plan them. Celebration does not need a holiday or formal designation. The ideas are seen as seeds for activities to be actually planned and designed by kids and adults working together. The unifying feature is a celebration of peace, life, and friendship.

Objectives

For Young Children:
- To choose some activities for a celebration.
- To cooperate with others in carrying out a large activity.

For Early Elementary Children:
- To plan cooperative and supportive activities for a celebration.
- To carry out pieces of a large activity responsibly.

For Later Elementary Children:
- To manage the planning and carrying out of a large celebration activity.
- To create original activities to be a part of a celebration event.

For All Children:
- To have fun together.
- To build hope.

Afternoon at the Parade

You Will Need:
- banners or streamers
- wagons
- dress-up clothes, make-up
- stuffed animals
- balloons
- popcorn
- rhythm instruments

What To Do:

1. Plan a parade! Think about what things you would like to have in your parade. Some ideas to consider are:
   - clowns;
   - popcorn;
   - "floats" (wagons with decorations);
   - animal acts;
   - people acts like baton twirlers, dancers, weight lifters, singers;
   - music.

2. Plan what needs to be done. You may want to have committees or work groups. Groups could work on:
   - dress-ups and make-up;
   - popcorn;
   - decorating floats;
   - organizing the animal and people acts;
   - making instruments (shakers made out of beans in containers, bells sewn on wrist bands, drums made out of cans with lids and sticks, kazoos from wax paper on the end of a paper towel roll or folded over a comb);
   - blowing up balloons; or
   - making signs.

3. When your parade is all ready, start marching and enjoy the parade!

Let's Talk About It:

Why are parades fun? What was the most fun about yours? What other parade ideas do you have?

Did you make sure everyone felt included and had important jobs?

Other Things To Do:

Go to a parade in your town. Maybe you could make a children's peace float to enter in your local parade.

Plan a parade or circus for your neighbors, senior citizen friends, or another group of children.

Backyard Fair

You Will Need:
- boxes   • blankets or sheets   • bean bags   • wheelbarrow or wagon
- jar and clothespins   • snacks   • balls   • flying disk
- card tables   • dress-up clothes and camera
- magnets, string, and pole

What To Do:
1. Plan a backyard fair. Think about fairs you have visited. Choose some of your favorite ideas for your fair.

2. Think about each idea you chose. Decide what things you will need for each idea. You could make:
- a tunnel of fun. Use cardtables, old sheets with windows cut out, balloons, and funny pictures.
- a bean bag toss. You need a container or board with a hole, and bean bags. They can be made out of socks with beans inside and tied or sewn at the open end.
- clothespins in a jar. A jar or milk jug with clothespins to drop in.
- wheelbarrow or wagon rides. Someone strong is needed to push or pull.
- ball toss. Have a basket or box and balls.
- flying disk toss. Have a box or hole to throw it through, or some way to measure how far people throw the flying disk.
- fish in the pond. Fix up a pole with string and a magnet on the end and paper "fish" with paper clips on them.
- dress-ups. Let people dress up and have their pictures taken with a pretend camera or a real one. Instant pictures are best.
- snack bar. Fix your favorite snacks!

3. Set up your fair. Have different booths for the different activities. If you think lots of people will come, you will need to have someone "in charge" at each booth.

Let's Talk About It:
What could you celebrate at your fair?

What other activities have you seen at fairs? Do any try to make fun for some by hurting others or teasing them? How can you change those activities to be fun for all? How can you set up your activities so that everyone wins?

Other Things To Do:

You may want to plan a fair or carnival that will help you make money to help meet the needs of your school or church or to make a donation to a group working for peace and justice.